D1129497

ARCHIMEDES
AND HIS
WONDERFUL
DISCOVERIES

ARCHIMEDES AND HIS WONDERFUL DISCOVERIES

ARTHUR JONAS

ILLUSTRATED BY ALIKI

PRENTICE-HALL, INC., ENGLEWOOD CLIFFS, N. J.

To the children of the Wilson School

Another Prentice-Hall book by the same author:
New Ways in Math
illustrated by Aliki

Archimedes and His Wonderful Discoveries
by Arthur Jonas

Copyright under International
and Pan–American copyright conventions

© 1963 by Prentice-Hall, Inc.,
Englewood Cliffs, N.J.

Library of Congress Catalog Card Number: 63-10247

Printed in the United States of America
04404-J (T)   04405-J (L)

CONTENTS

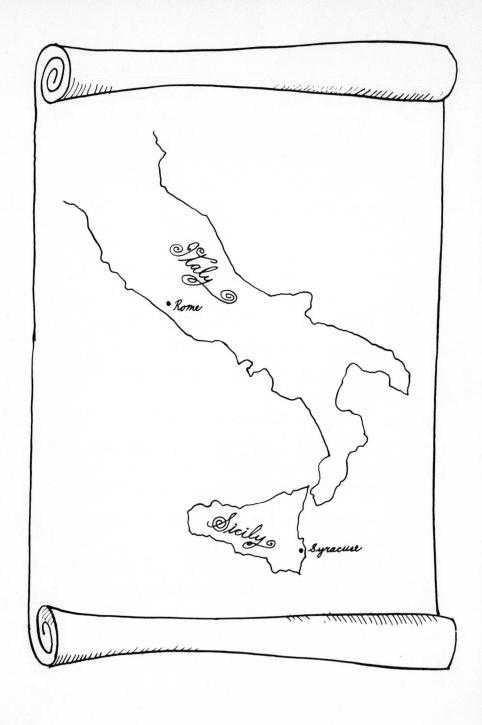

I.

THE EARLY DAYS

Did you ever write in the sand? Did you ever look at the stars and wonder how far away they are? Did you ever work so hard that you didn't hear someone call you? This is a book about the discoveries of a great scientist and mathematician named Archimedes (are-kih-MEE-deez). He did these things, too.

Archimedes was born in Syracuse in 287 B.C. Syracuse was a city on an island off the toe of Italy. The island is called Sicily. The people of Syracuse were Greek. At the time of Archimedes the Greeks were leaders in science, mathematics, writing, drama, music, and many other fields.

Almost all that we know about the life of Archimedes was written by people who lived long after his death. Some of the stories told about him may not be all true. We do know that Archimedes wrote many books. The books tell about his discoveries. He wrote very little about himself.

Archimedes wrote his books on long strips made of *papyrus* or parchment. Papyrus was made from sliced and pressed parts of the papyrus plant. Parchment was usually made from sheepskin. The strips of parchment or papyrus were rolled up on large spools. You see, Archimedes lived in the days before we had paper. There were no printing presses, either. Everything was written by hand. If you wanted a copy of a book, you could hire someone to copy it. The people who did the copying were called *scribes*.

The Greeks loved learning so much that their scribes were kept busy making copies of books. Some of the Greek books were brought to the seaport of Syracuse by trading ships. In this way, Archimedes was able to read the newest books from the mainland of Greece.

Archimedes was the son of Phidias (FID-ee-us), the astronomer. Almost nothing is known about the childhood of Archimedes. But we can guess that his family brought him up much as other Greek citizens brought up their children.

Archimedes' parents probably hung an olive branch on their door to announce his birth. Soon after he was born he was probably rubbed with oil by a family slave. Very likely his parents gave a large family party when he was ten days old and was given his name. The name Archimedes is a very unusual name. It means *chief thinker,* or *first rate,* or *master thinker.* Perhaps his father made it up hoping his son would make the name come true.

The main job of a Greek mother was raising the children. She was helped by the family slaves. At the age of eight, boys started school. School was held at the teacher's house. Students learned to write the letters of the alphabet and they learned how to use letters as numbers. They studied geometry and the rules for proving things to be true. They also learned about Greek writers like Homer and Aesop (EE-sop). Some of their time was spent in learning to play the lyre, which is a stringed instrument something like a harp.

Phidias wanted his son to have a good education. He sent Archimedes to study at the library in Alexandria, Egypt. Here Archimedes worked with the greatest scientists and mathematicians.

When Archimedes returned home to Syracuse, he worked as a mathematician and as a scientist. Because papyrus was expensive Archimedes did not use it until he felt satisfied that he had solved the problem he was working on. This meant that he had to find something else to use as scrap paper for his figuring, and he did.

Most of the time he did his figuring in the sand. Sometimes he would write in the ashes at the fireplace. He would even write numbers in the oil which was rubbed on his body when he took a bath. After he solved a problem he wrote it out on papyrus so that others could see what he had discovered.

There are those who say that when Archimedes worked on a problem he often forgot to eat or sleep. At times he even had to be dragged to the tub to take a bath. Does this sound like anyone you know?

King Hiero II (HY-er-o) of Syracuse was a relative of Archimedes. From time to time the king would call on Archimedes to help solve some hard problem. Archimedes preferred working on his own interests and usually did not want to be interrupted by the king. But since he liked the king very much, Archimedes often put his own work aside to help him.

II.

WAS THE CROWN
PURE GOLD?

King Hiero wanted a new gold crown. He had a lump of gold carefully weighed and ordered a goldsmith to make the crown. When the goldsmith finished the crown and took it to the king, the crown weighed exactly the same as the gold which the king had given to the goldsmith. The king was happy because he was certain that the goldsmith had put all the gold into the crown.

But after awhile the king began to have doubts about the honesty of the goldsmith. Perhaps the weight of the crown was too exact. King Hiero wondered if he had been cheated. Maybe the goldsmith had not put all the gold into the crown. Perhaps the goldsmith had kept some of the gold for himself and had used an equal weight of silver instead. The crown would look the same and weigh the same but it would not be worth the same as if it had been made of pure gold. This is because silver is less valuable than gold. Was the crown pure gold?

King Hiero called on Archimedes to help him decide whether he had been cheated. Archimedes thought and thought; then he thought some more. He could not find a way to tell if there was any silver in the crown, but he kept on thinking.

One day he went to the public baths. As he got into the tub he saw that the level of the water sloshed over the top of the tub. The overflowing water gave Archimedes an idea for solving the problem of the gold in the crown. He was so excited with his discovery that he ran through the streets shouting *eureka!* (you-REE-ka). This means *I have found it!* Archimedes was in such a hurry when he ran out of the bath that he forgot to put his clothes on.

This was Archimedes' idea: He knew that different materials had different weights. For example, if you have a piece of rock and a piece of wood exactly the same size, the rock will weigh more than the wood. The amount of room or space something occupies is called its *volume*. Archimedes had found a way to figure the volume of the king's crown without having to melt it down into a lump. He would put the crown into water just as he himself had been in the tub.

When Archimedes was in the tub he saw that he could use water to measure the volume, or displacement, of the crown and the lump of gold. You can see this for yourself when you step into a half-filled tub. As you step into the water, the level of the water rises. The more of you that is under the water, the more water you displace and the higher the level of the water. The water that you push out of the way is your *displacement*, or how much room your body takes up under water. If you try to see your displacement in a bathtub, be careful not to let the water overflow.

An easy way for Archimedes to find the displacement of the crown was to fill a clay jar to the brim with water and place the jar into a bowl to catch the overflow. Then he could measure the amount of overflow, or displacement. Archimedes also knew that he could measure the displacement of a lump of gold and the golden crown of the king. The lump of gold and the crown should displace the same amount of water if the crown was pure gold. But, if the goldsmith had taken part of the gold in the crown and put in an equal weight of any other metal, the displacement would *not* be the same.

Archimedes put the crown into the filled jar. Water overflowed. He measured the volume of the overflow. Next he put a lump of pure gold which weighed exactly the same as the crown into the water-filled jar. The water that spilled over the edge of the jar this time was less than when the crown had been used. Although the lump

of gold and the crown weighed exactly the same, the gold displaced less water. The gold took up less room than the crown. If the crown had been pure gold, it would have displaced exactly the same amount of water as the lump of gold. Since silver is lighter than gold a greater amount of silver is needed to weigh the same as gold. The extra silver caused the crown to take up more room than the pure gold. That is why it displaced more water. The king had been cheated. The crown was not pure gold.

III.

"ON FLOATING BODIES"

When he had solved the problem of the crown, Archimedes did not stop his work. He continued to experiment with other materials and liquids. As you have seen, different materials have different weights. If you take a piece of gold and a piece of silver that are both the same size, the piece of gold will weigh more than the piece of silver. Because gold is heavier than silver a pound of gold will take up less room or displace less water than a pound of silver. The heavier a material, the more *dense* it is. Gold is more dense than silver. Copper is less dense than silver. Density is a way of comparing weights of materials.

Archimedes found another way of comparing materials. He compared the weight of a material and the weight of the water it displaced. This gave a number called *specific gravity*. For example, a twenty-pound lump of gold will displace about one pound of water.

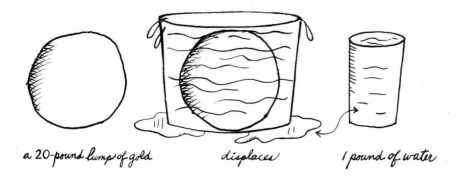

a 20-pound *lump of gold*   *displaces*   *1 pound of water*

This means that gold is twenty times heavier than water. Therefore, the specific gravity of gold is about 20. A ten-pound lump of silver will displace about one pound of water. Silver is ten times heavier than water. So the specific gravity of silver is about 10. Specific gravity is a very useful way of telling different things apart. It is often used by jewelers and other people who work with metal.

Liquids, too, have density. Some liquids are very heavy, like molasses. Some are very light, like gasoline. Salt water is more dense than fresh water. A quart of salt water weighs more than a quart of fresh water. The denser a liquid is, the easier it is to float in it. Did you ever go bathing in the ocean? It is easier to float in the ocean than in a lake. This is because the salt water of the ocean is more dense than the fresh water of a lake. But, if you go to the Great Salt Lake in Utah, the water is so dense that it is almost impossible to sink in it!

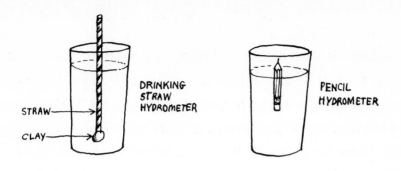

STRAW

CLAY

DRINKING
STRAW
HYDROMETER

PENCIL
HYDROMETER

You can show that salt water is denser than fresh water. Put an egg into a glass of fresh water. The egg will sink to the bottom of the glass. Now add a handful or two of salt to the water. Keep adding salt while you watch the egg. When enough salt has been added the egg will rise to the surface. You have shown that salt water is denser than an egg and that fresh water is not as dense as an egg. Therefore, an egg will float in dense salt water but will sink to the bottom in fresh water.

There is a way to measure the density of liquids. This is with a *hydrometer* (hy-DROM-ih-ter). A hydrometer floats. The higher up in the liquid the hydrometer floats, the more dense the liquid. You can make a hydrometer out of a short pencil or a weighted straw. Try the hydrometer in salt water and in fresh water. It should float higher in the salt water because salt water is more dense than fresh water.

We have seen that when an object is heavy enough to sink it displaces an amount of water equal to its volume.

21

Archimedes also studied things that float in water. He found that, when a ship is being loaded, it goes deeper and deeper into the water. As it gets heavier, it displaces more and more water. As long as the ship does not weigh more than the water it displaces, it will float. The weight of ships is measured by their displacement. The next time you are near a large ship notice the marks on its prow. These marks help to show how much cargo a ship can hold and how deep the ship can go into the water and still be safe.

When you swim did you ever notice that the water seems to hold you up? This push of the water is called *buoyancy* (BOO-yan-see). Archimedes found that floating things are buoyed up by a push equal to the weight of the water they displace. This idea is known today as Archimedes' Principle. Try pushing a ping-pong ball under water. It is *very* buoyant. A balloon filled with air is so buoyant that it is very hard to push it under water.

When you fill your lungs with air, you become more buoyant and you float more easily.

Archimedes found that there is even buoyancy when things do not float. He found that when things sink in water they become lighter. If a ball of iron weighed eight pounds out of water, it would weigh about seven pounds in water. This is because it displaces about a pound of water. Things that sink become lighter—as much lighter as the weight of the water they displace. You might want to use a spring scale to test the idea that things are lighter in water. The ideas that Archimedes discovered about water and things that float and sink were put into his book, *On Floating Bodies*. They were the beginning of what is now called *hydrostatics* (hy-dro-STAT-iks). These ideas are still used. Even something as modern as an atomic sub uses the discoveries of Archimedes.

The next time you take a bath, remember the many things Archimedes discovered by seeing that his body displaced water as he stepped into the tub. Perhaps you can see your displacement when you take a bath.

IV.

"I CAN MOVE THE EARTH"

How can a boy lift a man? If you have been on a
seesaw, you know the answer. A boy on one end of a
seesaw can lift a man on the other end if the man sits
near the center of the seesaw. When the boy lifts the
man on the seesaw, he is using the seesaw as a *lever*
(LEE-ver).

Just what is a lever? It is something that helps us to
do certain kinds of work more easily. A lever is a bar
which is free to move about a point. A seesaw is a bar.
It is free to move about a point or crossbar. The point
is called the *fulcrum* (FUL-krum). When you push or

pull on one end of the lever, you are using *force*. In return for the force you use on one end of the lever, the weight (or *resistance*) on the other end of the lever is moved. This moving is called *work*. Work, to a scientist, has to do with how much force (push or pull) is used and how far the weight (resistance) moves.

Much of what we know about levers was discovered by Archimedes. He found many ways to use levers. Archimedes was so pleased with his discoveries about levers that it is said he once told King Hiero, "Give me a place to stand on and I can move the earth." What a long lever he would have needed!

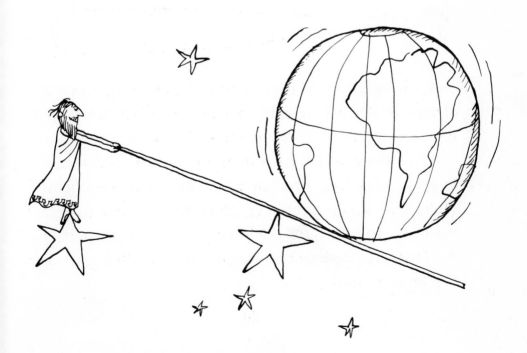

Today, we use levers in many ways:
A screwdriver is a lever.

A hammer is a lever.

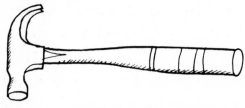

A baseball bat is a lever.

A wheelbarrow is a lever. So is a nutcracker, an oar of a rowboat, a fishing pole, a pickax, and a hatchet. Even your arm is a lever. Can you think of other levers?

All of these levers help us to do work. They all are made of some kind of a bar which moves about a point (fulcrum). You use force (push or pull) on one part of the lever. In return for the force you use on one part of the lever, the resistance (weight) on the other part of the lever is moved.

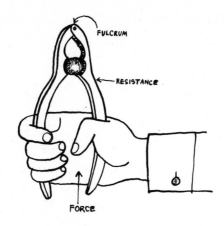

FULCRUM

RESISTANCE

FORCE

A 60-pound boy on the force end of a seesaw (lever) can use his 60 pounds to push hard enough to move a 120-pound woman on the resistance end of the seesaw (lever). To do this, the boy's end of the seesaw must be longer than the woman's end of the seesaw. The boy moves further than the woman. The boy is moving his 60 pounds over a longer distance in exchange for moving the 120-pound woman a shorter distance.

So the seesaw used as a lever helps the boy move the woman. The help that the seesaw gives is called *mechanical advantage*. Since the 60-pound boy can move the 120-pound woman, the mechanical advantage is 2. It is found by dividing 120 by 60. But to move the heavy woman, the boy had to move his end of the lever twice as far as the woman's end of the lever.

Try using a seesaw as a lever. You will discover many things. Can you lift your friends? Your parents? Your teacher? If you use a seesaw as a lever, you can. Perhaps you can try the seesaw during recess at school. You might even ask your teacher for extra recess so that you can study about levers.

Do you think Archimedes could really move the world if he had a long enough lever and a place to stand?

V.

SIX SIMPLE SERVERS

We have seen that a lever is a bar which is free to move on a point (a fulcrum). Force used on one part of the lever moves the weight on the other part of the lever and work is done.

Archimedes discovered other things about levers. He found that there are three ways that the force, fulcrum, and resistance can be arranged.

When you use a seesaw as a lever, the force is at one end, the resistance is at the other end, and the fulcrum is in between. This is a *first-class lever*. Other first-class

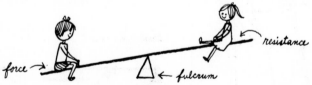

levers are scissors, a balance scale, and a crowbar. In all first-class levers the fulcrum is between the force and the resistance. Can you think of other first-class levers?

A wheelbarrow is a *second-class lever*. So is a nut-cracker, and an oar of a rowboat. In each second-class lever, the resistance is between the force and the fulcrum. Can you think of other second-class levers?

With a *third-class lever*, the fulcrum is at one end and the resistance is at the other end. The force is in between. A baseball bat is a third-class lever. So is a pair of tweezers, a broom, and even your arm. Can you see why?

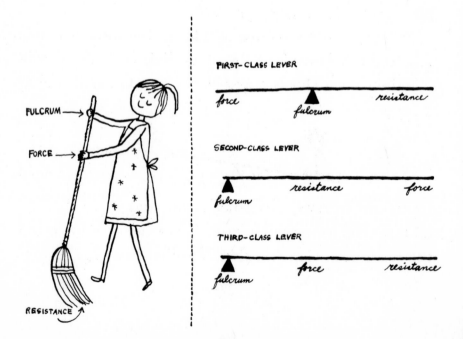

Not only did Archimedes discover many things about levers, but he also studied other simple *machines*. When you think of machines, perhaps you think of such things as a typewriter, a sewing machine, or a car. These modern machines are combinations of simple machines. There are really only six simple machines:

The *lever,* about which you already know, is a simple machine.

The *pulley,* which is a kind of lever, is also a simple machine. You can make a pulley out of a spool and a wire hanger. With two friends you can make a block

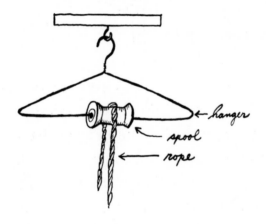

and tackle made up of several pulleys. You will need some clothesline. You will also need two broom handles. Tie the clothesline to one of the broom handles and wrap it around both handles, as shown in the picture.

When you wrap the line around the broom handles, you are making some pulleys. Ask your two friends to pull as hard as they can on the broom handles. If you pull on the rope, you can easily pull the two handles together.

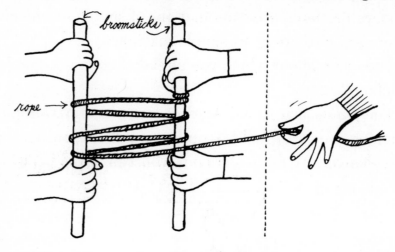

Archimedes used pulleys and levers to move a fully-loaded ship all by himself. King Hiero must have been surprised to see this! Wouldn't you have been?

Pulleys are very useful to us today. They can be used to move cars and elevators, to raise flags and Venetian blinds, and to work power-shovels. You can think of many other ways in which we use pulleys.

The *wheel and axle,* which is a kind of lever, is also a simple machine. You can make one out of a pencil sharpener. Take off the cover. Be careful not to spill any of the shavings. Tie a string tightly around the axle.

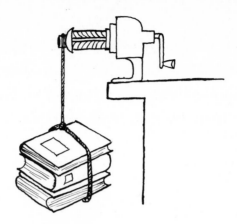

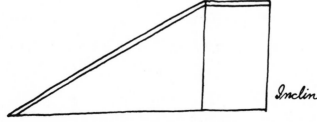

wheel and axle

To the other end of the string, tie a weight. You might try some books. As you turn the crank, the books are lifted. The force needed to turn the handle is much less than the weight of the books. Why do you think this is so? We use wheels and axles in many ways. The steering wheel of a car, a doorknob, the handle of a faucet, a wrench, and an eggbeater are examples of wheels and axles. Can you think of others?

The *inclined plane* is another kind of simple machine. This is the way it helps us to do work: If you have to lift a heavy weight, it is easier to push it up a slanted board than it is to lift it straight up. The slanted board is an inclined plane. Some trucks carry planks or in-

Inclined Plane

clined planes to help with the loading. Have you ever noticed that roads that go up mountains are often not straight? They wind around to avoid being too steep. This is another example of the use of the inclined plane.

Wedge

The *wedge,* which is really two inclined planes put together, is another useful simple machine. An ax or a hatchet is a wedge. When pins, nails, and needles are pushed through things, they are wedges.

The *screw* is also a simple machine. There are those who say that, while walking on the beach, Archimedes found a large screw-shaped shell. This gave him the idea for his screw.

The screw is an inclined plane wrapped around a cylinder. A meat grinder is a screw. Have you ever seen one? Have you ever seen a corkscrew? A drill? Archimedes put a screw inside a tube. He used it for raising

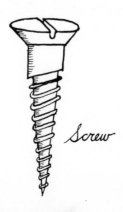

Screw

water. It came in handy for taking water out of boats and for watering plants on dry land. The *Archimedean screw* is still used to water dry land in parts of Egypt.

Sometimes many machines are used together. Look at a bicycle. Does the bicycle have any of the six simple machines? Can you find a lever? A wheel and axle?

As you can see from the use we make of machines today (pulleys, wheelbarrows, levers, bikes), the discoveries that Archimedes made over two thousand years ago help us with our work even though we live in the space age.

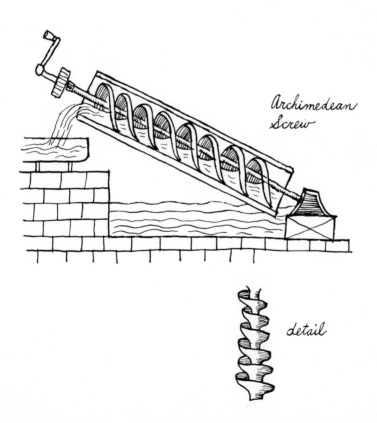

Archimedean Screw

detail

VI.

HOW IS YOUR BALANCE?

Did you ever watch a circus high-wire act? You may have seen a man walking on a high wire holding a long pole. The pole helps the man keep his balance.

Archimedes studied balance. He saw that things have a point where they balance.

Can you balance a stick on your fingers? Try balancing a fork, a pencil, a spoon, and a ruler.

Can you find the point of balance on these objects? Did you notice a point around which all the weight seems to center? This is the balance point or the *center of gravity*.

Archimedes found that the center of gravity is not always in the middle. A fork and a spoon are heavier on one end than on the other. Their centers of gravity are closer to the heavy end. Try balancing a baseball bat. Can you see that the center of gravity is not always in the middle?

There are many ways you can work with centers of gravity. Try using a piece of clay or a raw potato, a pencil, and a fork. Push the point of the pencil through the potato as shown in the picture. Then put the fork into

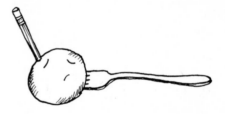

the potato. You may have to move the fork until the whole thing is balanced on the table. Give the end of the pencil a tap. It will go back and forth. Can you see the center of gravity?

Try using two forks, a pencil, and a potato, as shown in the picture. Can you balance them on top of a soda bottle? Where is the center of gravity?

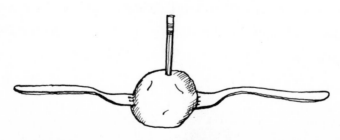

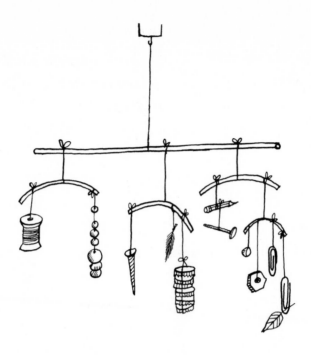

Did you ever make a mobile? If you want to make one, you will need some small objects, thread, and some sticks. If you start from the bottom and work up, you will see many things about the center of gravity.

You may see what Archimedes saw. If you tie equal weights to the stick, they will balance at equal distances. If one weight is heavier, its end of the stick will be lower. To balance the unequal weights you will have to move the heavier weight closer to the balance point or move the lighter weight further away from the balance point. Does this remind you of a lever?

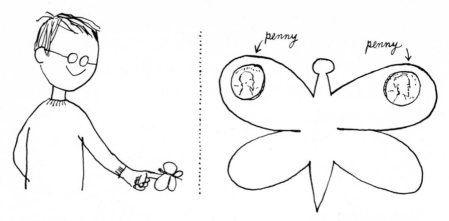

Look at the picture of the boy with the butterfly balanced on his finger. How does the butterfly stay on his finger? Perhaps you have guessed that the center of gravity is over the finger. On the underside of each front wing, a penny has been taped. Because of the weight of the pennies, the center of gravity is over the finger. You may want to make your own butterfly. Use a stiff piece of paper or cardboard.

Have you ever seen a roly-poly doll? Sometimes they are called topsy-turvy dolls. The doll will not tip over. This is because there is a heavy weight at the bottom of the doll. The weight makes the center of gravity very low.

The lower the center of gravity, the harder it is to tip something over.

The man on the circus high wire carries a long pole because it helps to lower his center of gravity. This keeps him from tipping over.

When a football lineman crouches, he lowers his center of gravity. He is harder to tip over.

A truck can stand on the side of the hill if its center of gravity is low enough.

When Archimedes made his discoveries about the centers of gravity, he started the science of mechanics. Without the science of mechanics there would be no automobiles, no airplanes, and no steamships.

VII.

MOVING PLANETS
AND FIXED STARS

The Greeks were very interested in astronomy. Many of them thought that the sky was a globe made of a substance like glass. They thought that the stars were attached to the sky. The Greeks had no telescopes but with their eyes they could see five stars that moved in the sky. They called these stars *planets*, which means *wanderers*. The five planets were Mercury, Venus, Mars, Jupiter, and Saturn. The Greeks thought that the sun and the moon were planets, too.

Greek astronomers knew that the moon shone by reflected sunlight. Some of them had the idea that the earth was round because they could see the curved shadow that the earth made on the moon.

The Greeks could see that the planets, the sun, and the moon moved. But they found it hard to explain why the planets moved when the stars stood still. It seemed to the Greeks that the planets did not travel in a straight line. If they observed a planet night after night for a year, the planet seemed to go back and forth in little circles as it moved across the sky. The motion of the planets was one of the problems that Greek astronomers tried hard to solve.

To help solve the problem, the Greeks made up a theory about the planets. A good theory is supposed to explain things. If the planet theory worked, they could tell in advance where a certain planet should be. To figure out things in advance is called *predicting*. The Greeks made up theories to predict and explain the motion of the planets.

One theory stated that the planets moved around the earth. This seemed to make sense because the sun and the moon look as if they revolve around the earth. But the theory did not explain the path that the planets take when they move.

Another theory stated that the planets moved around the earth but that the earth was not in the center. This did not explain the motion of the planets too well, either.

Some Greek astronomers came up with the idea that the planets go around the sun and the sun goes around the earth.

One astronomer even said that the earth and the planets go around the sun.

Most Greek astronomers thought that the earth was the center of the universe. They believed that the sun, the moon, and the planets went around the earth. Archimedes was interested in the many different theories on the motion of the planets. He even wrote about some of the theories in his book, *The Sand Reckoner*. As you remember, Archimedes' father was an astronomer. No doubt, father and son spent many hours discussing the heavens.

Archimedes built a model of the sun and the planets, which ran by water power. The model was made of glass balls or *spheres*. The spheres were placed inside each other. Each sphere held a different planet. The machine worked so well that it was able to predict the eclipses of the moon and the sun. Archimedes wrote a book about his model. The book is called *On Sphere Making* but it has been lost. Many years after Archimedes died, the Roman orator Cicero (SIS-ur-oh) saw Archimedes' model and wrote about it.

Archimedes did not have many tools to help him observe the stars. He used sundials, peepholes, and rods. He measured shadows and angles. He used what he

knew of mathematics. Sometimes he was very close to modern thinking. Sometimes he was far away.

His model of the planets was very close to the way they are.

On the other hand, he thought that the earth was ten times larger than it really is.

Archimedes thought that the sun was thirty times larger than the moon. Today we know that the sun is about four hundred times wider than the moon. He thought that the universe was much smaller than we know it to be. If Archimedes had had the telescopes, radar, and some of the other tools that we have today, there is no telling what he might have discovered about the universe.

45

People who work to discover new things are bound to make some mistakes. Mistakes are a part of discovering. When theories are used to help explain what we see and to make predictions, sooner or later we will know whether we have made a mistake. This is because we can test the predictions and see if they really happen. If the prediction does not come true, we look for the reason. Sometimes the theory needs to be changed. Sometimes the person testing the theory needs more training or better tools. At any rate, making up theories and testing them helps us to increase our knowledge. This is what Archimedes tried to do and this is what modern scientists try to do.

VIII.

SAND AND NUMBERS

What is the very largest number you know? A thousand? A million? A billion? No matter what number you can think of, there is a larger number. You can add one to any number to make it larger. There is no end to the amount of numbers there are. But, before the time of Archimedes, people did not know very much about large numbers.

The Greeks had not developed numerals for writing numbers. They used the letters of their alphabet to stand for numbers. There were twenty-seven letters in their alphabet. The largest numeral the Greeks had was a *myriad* (MEAR-ih-uhd). This was 10,000. They had no way of writing larger numbers.

Archimedes was not content to stop at the numeral 10,000 so he made up a problem for himself that would require the use of very large numbers and a way to write them. He set out to find a number that was larger than the number of grains of sand it would take to fill the universe.

To solve the problem Archimedes had to know how large the universe was. If you wanted to know how many apples were in a basket, you would have to know the size of the basket and how large the apples were. An easy way to do this would be to count the apples you put into the basket until it was filled.

Archimedes was not able to fill the universe with sand grain by grain, so he had to figure out its size by measuring a grain of sand and imagining how many grains it would take to fill the universe.

This is what Archimedes did: He put grains of sand side by side until there were enough to go across a poppy seed. Forty poppy seeds placed side by side made one *fingerbreadth*. Ten thousand fingerbreadths made one *stadium*. A stadium was about 600 feet long. This is as long as two football fields placed end-to-end. Archimedes used his knowledge of astronomy and mathematics to guess that the distance across the universe is 10,000,000,000 *stadia* (the plural of stadium). He figured that the number of grains of sand needed to fill the universe is 10 with 62 zeros after it. Try writing this number. It takes quite a while, doesn't it?

10, 000,000, 000, 000, 000,
   000, 000, 000, 000, 000,
   000, 000, 000, 000, 000,
   000, 000, 000, 000, 000, 00 *grains of sand.*

To count the grains of sand, Archimedes had to find a way to write large numbers. This is what he did: Archimedes multiplied numbers by themselves. When a number is multiplied by itself over and over again, the answer is called a *power*.

Here are some powers of 2:

$$2 = 2 \quad \text{1st power}$$
$$2 \times 2 = 4 \quad \text{2nd power}$$
$$2 \times 2 \times 2 = 8 \quad \text{3rd power}$$
$$2 \times 2 \times 2 \times 2 = 16 \quad \text{4th power}$$

Here are some powers of 3:

$$3 = 3 \quad \text{1st power}$$
$$3 \times 3 = 9 \quad \text{2nd power}$$
$$3 \times 3 \times 3 = 27 \quad \text{3rd power}$$
$$3 \times 3 \times 3 \times 3 = 81 \quad \text{4th power}$$

There is a short way to write a number to a power. 3^4. This is read: "three to the fourth power." The long way it is:

$$3 \times 3 \times 3 \times 3 = 81.$$

The little number which tells the power is called an *exponent*. In 5^4 the little ^{4} is an exponent. It means 5 to the fourth power, or 5 multiplied by itself four times.

$$5 \times 5 \times 5 \times 5 = 625.$$

Can you see that 5^4 is a short way to write 625?

5^5 is a short way to write 3,125. Check the answer.

$$
\begin{aligned}
5 &= 5 &\text{or } 5^1\\
5 \times 5 &= 25 &\text{or } 5^2\\
5 \times 5 \times 5 &= 125 &\text{or } 5^3\\
5 \times 5 \times 5 \times 5 &= 625 &\text{or } 5^4\\
5 \times 5 \times 5 \times 5 \times 5 &= 3,125 &\text{or } 5^5
\end{aligned}
$$

Any number can be multiplied by itself. 5^2 is five to the second power or:

$$5 \times 5 = 25.$$

5^3 is five to the third power or:

$$5 \times 5 \times 5 = 125.$$

The numbers 2 and 5 were too small for Archimedes to use. Instead he started with a myriad, which, as you know, is 10,000. Archimedes multiplied a myriad by itself. Then he multiplied it by itself again. He was using powers of a myriad just as we used powers of 2 or 5. By multiplying myriads by themselves, Archimedes was able to write as large a number as he pleased. He could write a number larger than the grains of sand it would take to fill the universe. He could even write a number larger than all the atoms in the universe!

Archimedes wrote a book about the grains of sand and large numbers. The book is called *The Sand Reckoner*. In the first part of the book, Archimedes writes about the size of the universe. He explains some of the ideas of the Greek astronomers. You might enjoy reading part of *The Sand Reckoner*, or having it read to you.

The next time you are at the seashore or near sand, try counting some of the grains. Even a small handful will add up to a very large number. Yet, no matter how large the number turns out to be, Archimedes showed that there is no end to numbers. They go on and on and on . . .

three million and ninety-one . . .
three million and ninety-two . . .

IX.

WAR AND MACHINES

Archimedes lived most of his life in a time of peace. But when he was an old man in his seventies war began to rage near Syracuse.

The war was between two great cities, Rome and Carthage. Each city wanted to rule the Mediterranean Sea on which their trading ships sailed. If you look at the map, you can see that poor little Syracuse was right between Rome and Carthage.

Under King Hiero, Syracuse was friendly with Rome. But King Hiero was an old man. When he died, his grandson became king but not for long. Soon a man named Hippocrates (hih-POK-ruh-teez) killed the grandson. Hippocrates was a friend of Carthage. He fought against the Romans. He told the people of Syracuse that the Romans were cruel. The people believed him and asked Hippocrates to be their leader and protect them. This meant that Syracuse was no longer on the side of Rome but was now on the side of Carthage *against* Rome.

Marcellus (mar-SELL-us) was the Roman general in command. He moved his army to Syracuse. He had sixty galleys and each galley had five rows of oars. He had

A Roman Galley

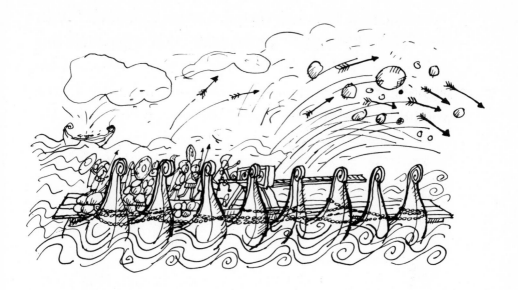

many kinds of arms and missiles. The Romans chained
eight ships together. They placed long planks across
the ships. On the planks they had a large engine which
could throw stones and darts. Against such weapons,
ships, and men, how could little Syracuse, even with its
stone wall, defend itself?

However, Syracuse had something that the Romans
did not have. It had Archimedes! King Hiero had talked
Archimedes into inventing some machines that could
be used to defend Syracuse if war should come. Now
King Hiero was dead. But the machines of Archimedes
were ready. Could they stand up against the might of
Rome?

Archimedes directed the use of his machines. With great accuracy and a lot of noise they threw arrows and stones at the Romans. The Roman soldiers were frightened. Large levers were used to drop heavy weights on the Roman ships. Many of them sank.

Archimedes used levers and pulleys to attach iron claws to the prows of the Roman galleys. By pulling on ropes the soldiers of Syracuse were able to lift the prows of the galleys. Some galleys were even picked up out of the water and dashed against the cliffs.

Mirrors were used to reflect the sun's light on the Roman ships. By carefully moving the mirrors Archimedes was able to reflect enough light to set the ships on fire.

The Roman stone-throwing machines were no match for the machines of Archimedes. Archimedes' machines were so accurate that the Romans did not dare to get too close and finally decided to sail away. The Roman army which had marched too close to the walls of Syracuse had also felt the power of Archimedes and retreated.

The Romans were no match for the machines of Archimedes at long range. So they decided to creep up to the wall at night and fight at close range. But Archimedes was ready for them. He had made short-range machines. These machines fired stones and arrows through little holes in the city wall. Once again the Romans had to retreat. As they withdrew, the long-range machines of Archimedes were again used. They did a lot of damage to the Romans.

Days and weeks passed. Whenever the Romans came too close to the walls of Syracuse, the machines of Archimedes would drive them back. The Romans became so afraid of Archimedes that, if they saw a piece of wood or rope on top of the wall, they would cry, "There it is. Archimedes is training some engine upon us." Then the Romans would run away.

For three years the machines of Archimedes held off the Romans. The army of Syracuse was safe behind the wall.

From time to time the men of Syracuse and the Romans would stop fighting to trade prisoners. During one of these meetings, the Roman general, Marcellus, noticed that at one place along the wall there were very few guards.

One night, as the people of Syracuse were celebrating a holiday, a small band of Romans crept over the wall. They spread out through the city. In the morning the Romans blew trumpets from many different parts of the city. The people of Syracuse thought that the whole Roman army was inside their walls. They ran in fright. Then the Romans opened the gates and let their whole army in. Syracuse was lost.

It was the custom for soldiers who captured a city to take anything they wanted. This was called *plundering*.

Marcellus gave orders that Archimedes was not to be harmed. During the plundering, however, Archimedes was killed. This sad event happened in 212 B.C. when he was seventy-five years old. There are those who say that Archimedes was alone working on a problem in the sand. A Roman soldier came up and ordered Archimedes to follow him to Marcellus. Archimedes was so busy that he did not hear the soldier. The Roman became angry and killed Archimedes.

Others say that Archimedes was working in the sand and that a Roman soldier drew his sword. Archimedes asked the soldier not to disturb him until he had finished his problem. The soldier did not understand and killed Archimedes.

Marcellus was very upset by the death of Archimedes. He saw to it that Archimedes had a fine funeral. Archimedes was buried in a grave that was marked by the figure of a sphere inside a cylinder.

However it happened, the greatest mathematician of the ancient world was dead and Syracuse was destroyed. Like so many other wars, this one resulted in waste, destruction, and death.

X.

THE PIECES OF A PUZZLE

Many important men write books about themselves. These books are called *autobiographies*. Often, other people write books about great men. These books are called *biographies*. When we want to know about the lives of great men, we can turn to these books. But we do not have any books about Archimedes that were written by people who met him and he wrote almost nothing about himself.

Archimedes did write books about his discoveries but to learn about his life we have to go to other writers. The trouble is that the oldest books we have about Archimedes were written many years after his death. From these books we learn the stories or legends that were told about Archimedes.

A *legend* is a story that has been handed down from father to son. Most legends tell about wonders or great deeds. As the stories are told and retold, they are some-

times changed. By the time the legend is written down, it may be quite different from the original story.

The discoveries of Archimedes were wonders. Many people told stories and legends about them and the inventor of these marvels. Some of the stories were written down many years later.

To find out about the life of Archimedes, the many stories that were written about him have to be put together like a jigsaw puzzle.

Here are some of the pieces:

From John Tzetzes (TSET-seez) we learned that Archimedes was seventy-five years old when he died; but John Tzetzes was born more than one thousand years after Archimedes' death.

The *eureka* story in which Archimedes is said to have run through the streets without his clothes on is from the writings of a Roman named Vitruvius (vih-TRUE-vee-us). This, too, was written long after Archimedes died.

About five hundred years after Archimedes' death, Papus (PAY-pus) wrote that Archimedes said, "Give me a place to stand on, and I can move the earth." Papus also wrote about Archimedes' work on levers and spheres.

Two hundred years after Archimedes died, a Greek named Diodorus (dy-o-DO-rus) wrote that Archimedes had studied in Alexandria, Egypt.

Cicero was born about one hundred years after Archimedes died. Cicero wrote that he saw the model of the sun, the moon, and the planets that Archimedes had built. He also wrote that he had seen Archimedes' grave which was marked by a sphere inside a cylinder.

Ptolemy (TOL-ih-me) and Lucian (LU-shun) lived about three hundred years after Archimedes.

Ptolemy wrote about Archimedes' work in astronomy.

Lucian, a Greek, explained how Archimedes had set fire to the Roman galleys by using mirrors.

The Roman historian, Plutarch (PLU-tark), wrote in detail about the gallant defense of Syracuse. Plutarch lived two hundred years after Archimedes but, because of Plutarch, more is known of Archimedes' death than his life. Most of the last chapter you have just read on the war machines is based on Plutarch's writings.

It is interesting to note that Plutarch did not really concern himself with Archimedes. Plutarch was interested in writing about the Roman general Marcellus. Today the main thing that we remember about Marcellus is that one of his soldiers killed Archimedes.

If little is known about the day to day life of Archimedes, much is known about his discoveries. Archimedes left many books. He wrote about:

floating bodies
levers
figures
numbers
centers of gravity
circles

and many other things. But he did not write about war machines even though he did so much with them to help defend Syracuse.

Some of Archimedes' books have been lost. From time to time one of his lost books is found. Perhaps more will be found in the future. Someday a book may even be found that will tell us more about his life.

We do know enough to say that Archimedes was a genius. He was modern in the way he made his discoveries. He did not work the way most of the Greek mathematicians did.

The Greek mathematicians tried to solve their problems by using only a compass and a ruler. The ruler was used for drawing straight lines. The compass was used for drawing circles. Greek mathematicians were not

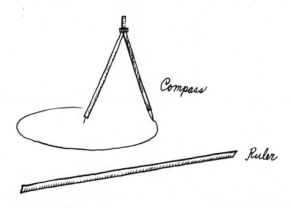

supposed to try things out. They were only to use their minds. As a result, they sometimes did not know when they were making a mistake in their thinking.

Archimedes used any way he could find to solve problems. He noticed things and tried to explain them. He conducted experiments. His use of levers and pulleys to move a ship is an example of the way he put his discoveries into practice.

Archimedes was a giant—both as a scientist and as a mathematician. Many of his discoveries, although over two thousand years old, are still used today. Perhaps two thousand years from now people will still be using the discoveries of Archimedes.

INDEX

P·H
JUNIOR
RESEARCH
BOOKS

WINTER-SLEEPERS by Phyllis Sarasy
 Hibernation patterns and habits of animal sleepers.

THE MAGIC OF WORDS by Arthur Alexander
 From picture-writing to secret codes, the development of language.

TELEVISION AND HOW IT WORKS by Eugene David
 The television program, how it is received on your set, and how each step works.

IN THE DEEP BLUE SEA by Elizabeth Morgan
 Mysteries of the sea including ocean-mining, oil-drilling, harvesting of ocean crops.

THINGS THAT MEASURE by Philip B. Carona
 The complete story of measuring from a crude cubit to modern instruments of the space age.

GO! THE STORY OF OUTER SPACE by Charles Spain Verral
 Man's past, present and future in outer space.

COMPUTERS AT YOUR SERVICE by Bernice Kohn
 How the computer was invented; how it works, what its present uses are.

THE HIDDEN YOU: Psychology In Your Life by Arthur Alexander
 The story of the mind. Simple explanations of the hidden self.

JETS by Charles Spain Verral
 Jets, their history and how the four leading types of engines work and why.

OUR TINY SERVANTS: Molds and Yeasts by Bernice Kohn
 Explains everyday wonders of molds and yeasts—how they help and harm us.

NEW WAYS IN MATH by Arthur Jonas
 From bartering to present binary number systems, flip flop circuits.

GIANT ANIMALS OF LONG AGO by Agnes McCarthy
 The kinds of giant animals and fish; their habits and habitats.

MAGIC MIXTURES: Alloys and Plastics by Philip B. Carona
 How these fields play an important role in our lives.

THE PEACEFUL ATOM by Bernice Kohn
 The development of peaceful uses of the atom from the pre-atomic era to the present.

ROBERT GODDARD: Father Of The Space Age by Charles Spain Verral
 The life of Robert Goddard, inventor of the liquid fuel rocket.

SOUNDS YOU CANNOT HEAR by Eric Windle
 The world of ultrasonics told in the language of a young reader.

TOOLS OF THE SCIENTIST by Rhoda Goldstein
 History and use of science "tools" including telescope, microscope, atom smasher.

WHO DO YOU THINK YOU ARE? The Story Of Heredity by Marguerite Rush Lerner, M. D.
 An historical survey and timely report on heredity.

WILDLIFE TEAMS by Natalie Friendly
 The "living together" of plants and animals described in simple and familiar terms.